AROUND TOWN

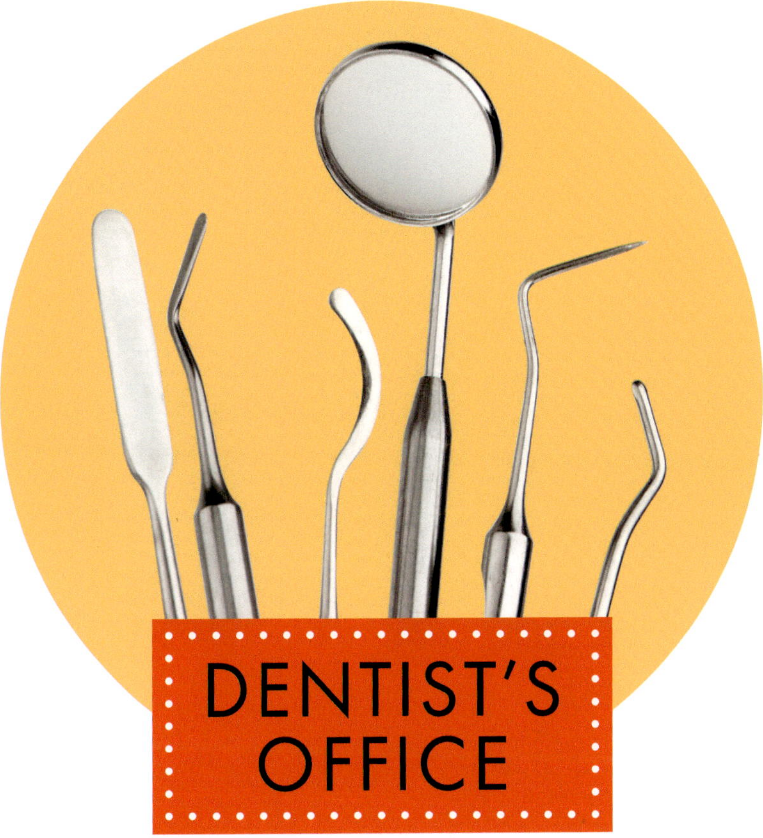

DENTIST'S OFFICE

by Susan Rose Simms

bib

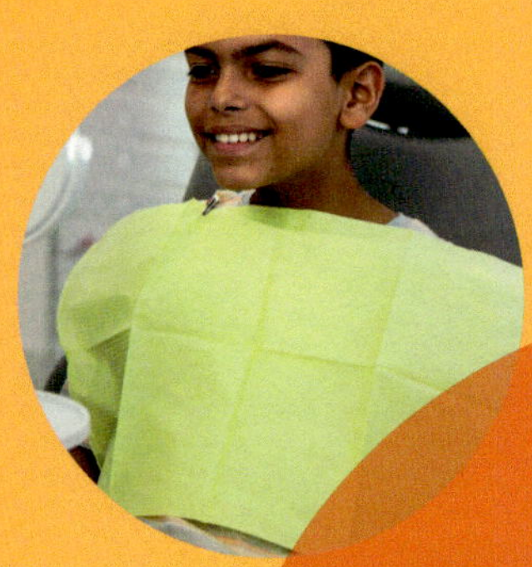

tools

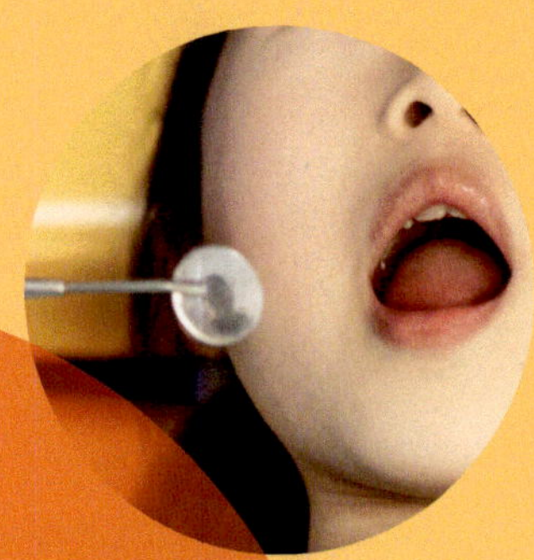

Look for these words and pictures as you read.

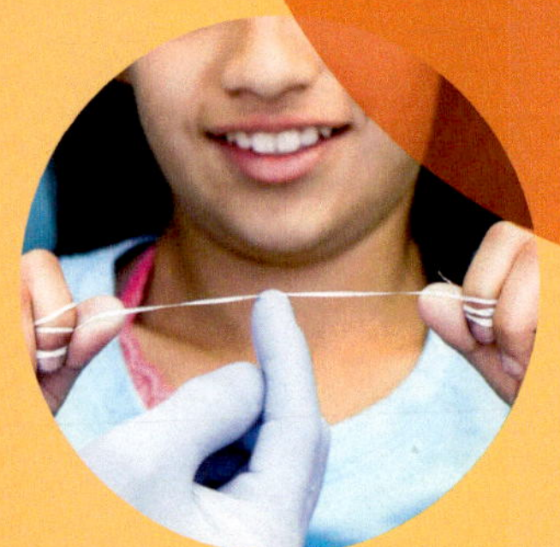

floss

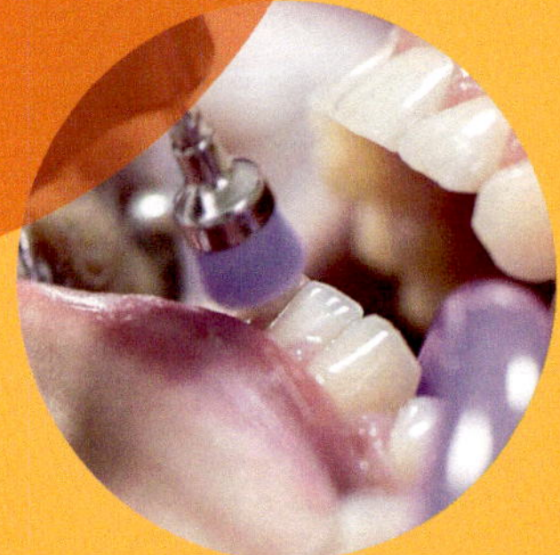

polish

Let's go to the dentist's office.
What will we see?

bib

Look at the bib.
It clips on.
It keeps Asa dry.

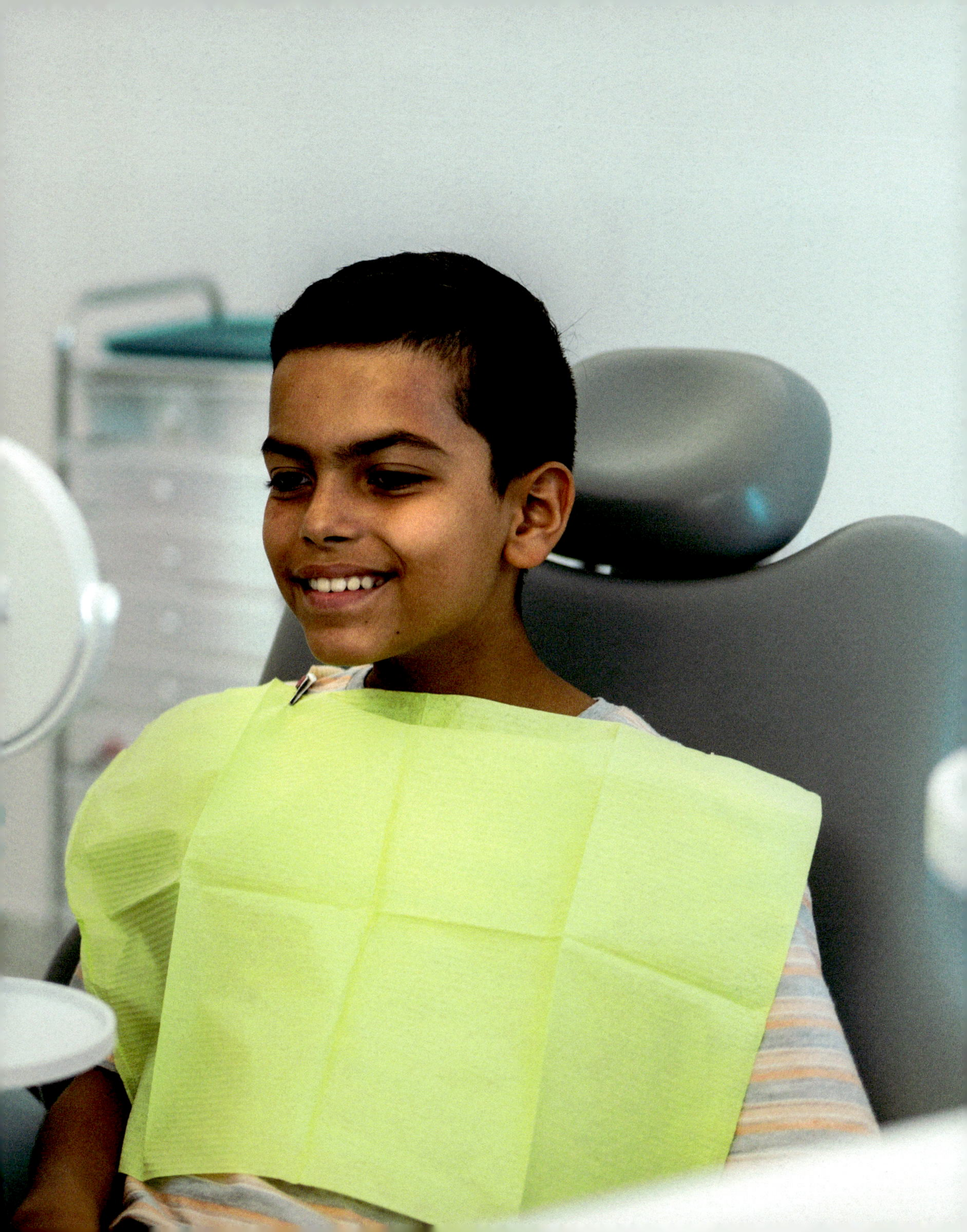

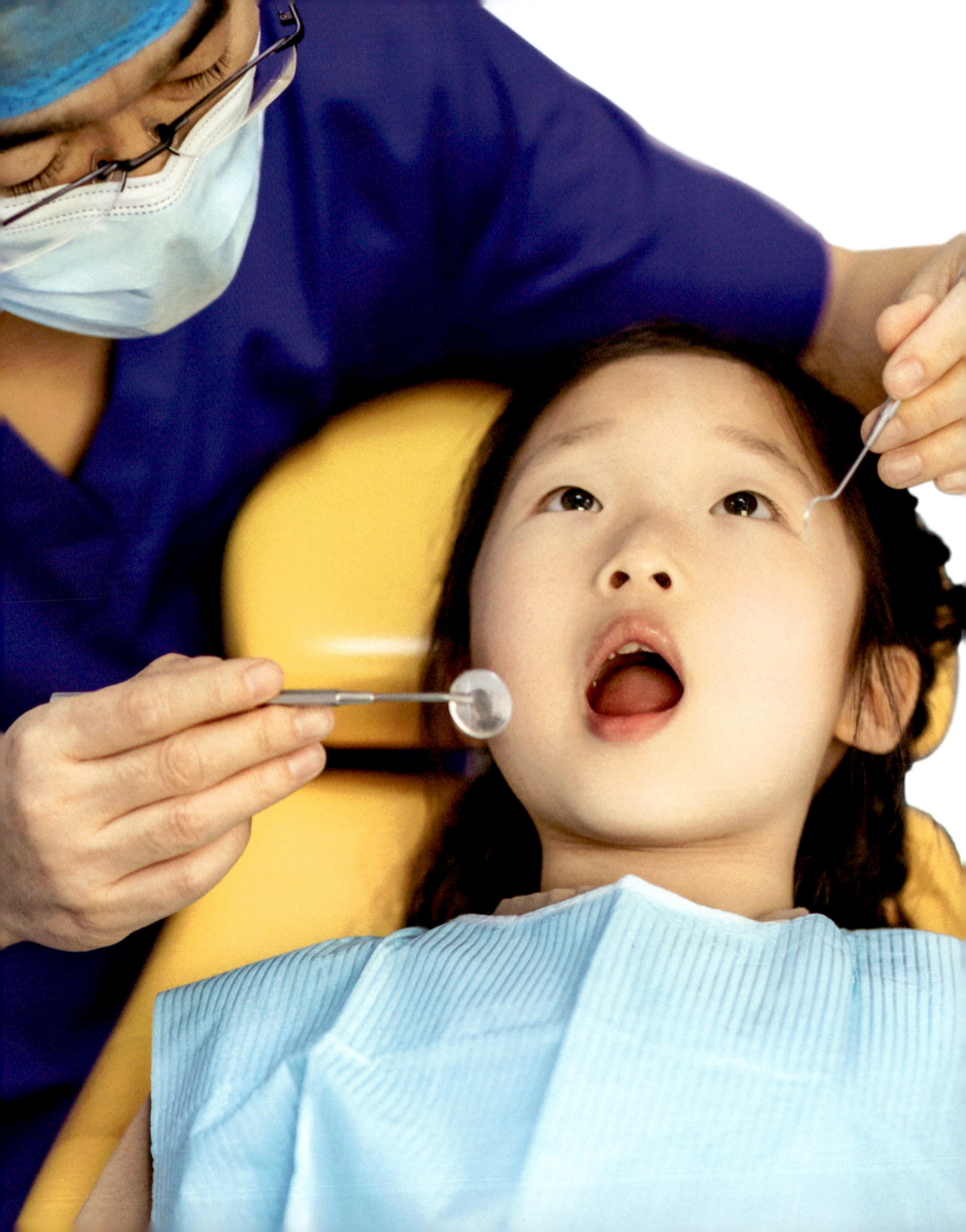

tools

Look at the tools.

One is a mirror.

Say ahh!

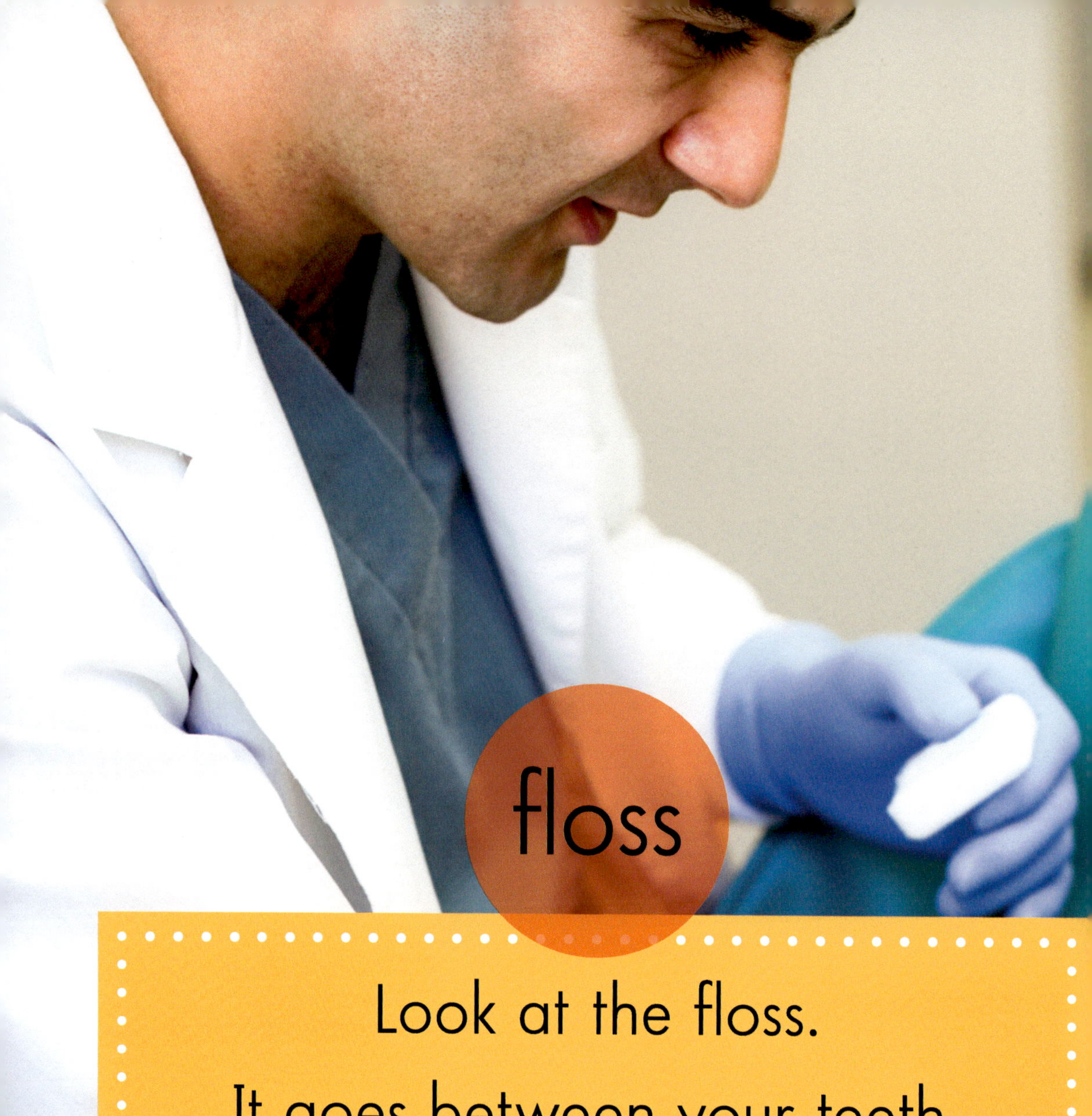

floss

Look at the floss.
It goes between your teeth.
Flossing keeps your gums healthy.

polish

Look at the polish.
It cleans your teeth.
It makes them shine.

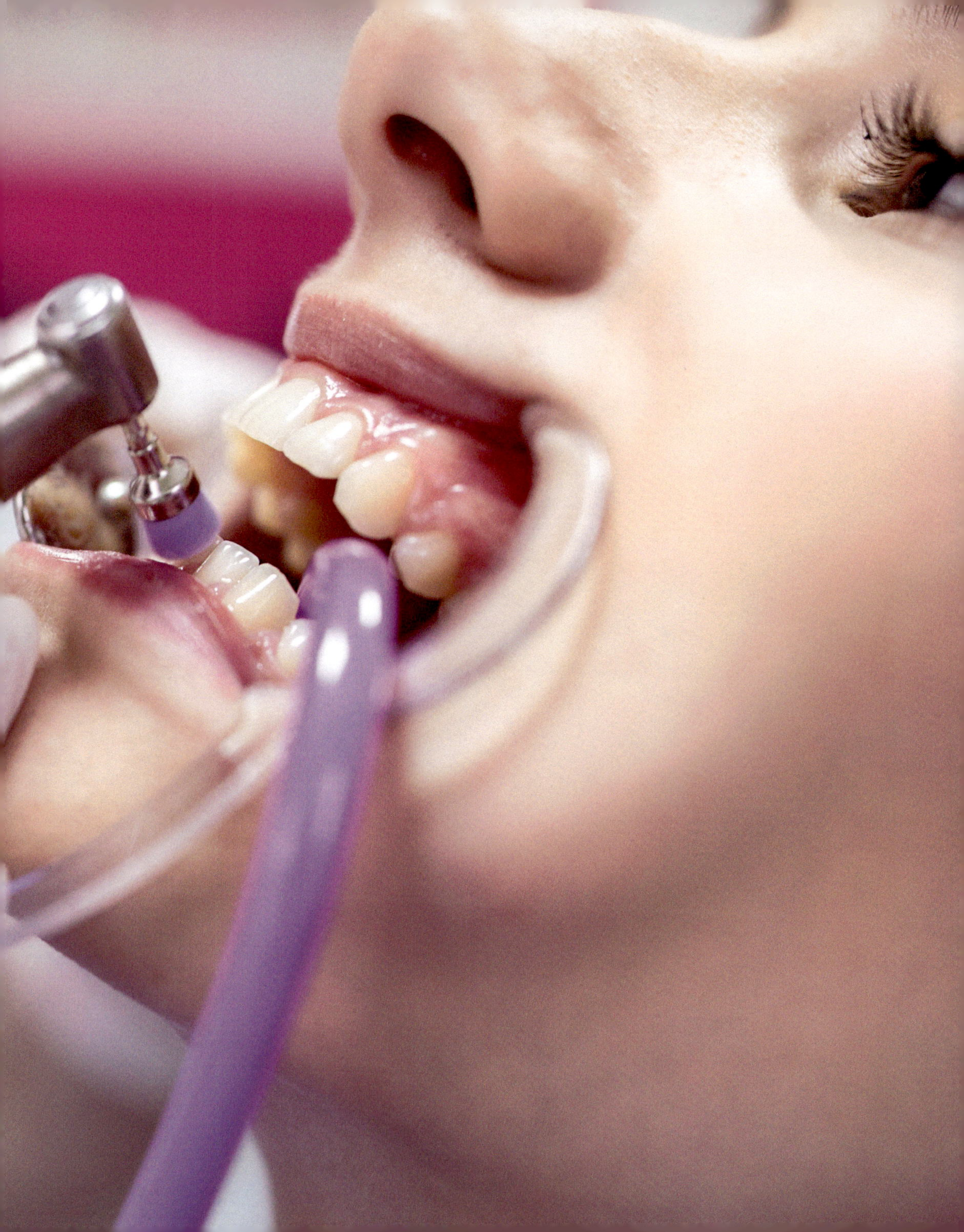

People wait in the lobby.
It is almost Kai's turn.

The dentist helps everyone.
Then he goes home.
He'll be back tomorrow.

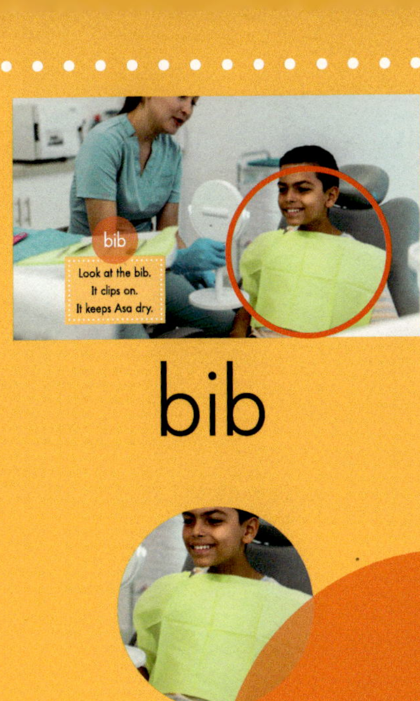

bib

tools

Did you find?

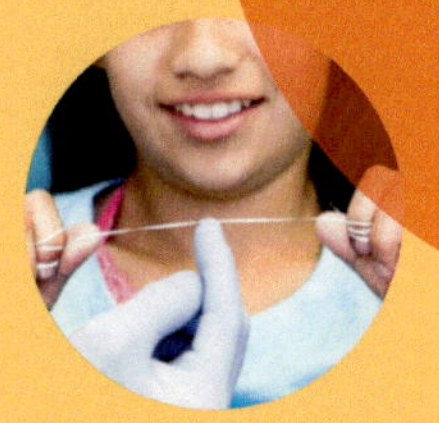

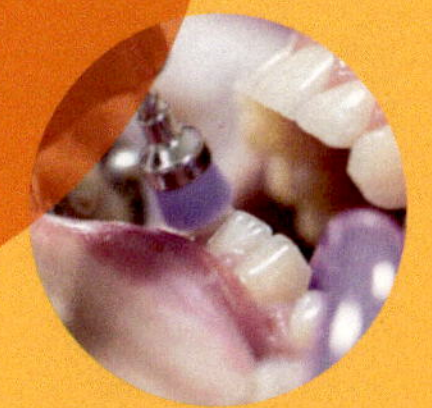

floss

polish

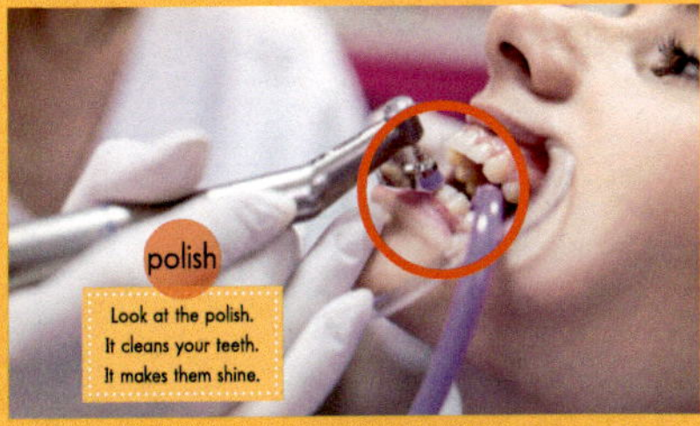

Spot is published by Amicus Learning, an imprint of Amicus
P.O. Box 227, Mankato, MN 56002
www.amicuspublishing.us

Cataloging-in-Publication data is available
from the Library of Congress.
Library Binding ISBN: 9798892008242
Paperback ISBN: 9798892008907
eBook ISBN: 9798892009560

LCCN: 2025012845

Ana Brauer, editor
Deb Miner, series designer
Sara Hood, book designer
and photo researcher

Photos by Dreamstime/Ellobo1, cover, 16; Getty Images/Bill Varie, 2, 8–9, 15, Dobrila Vignjevic, 2, 10–11, 15, FG Trade Latin, 2, 4–5, 15, Lorado, 3, Maskot, 12–13, owngarden, 2, 6, 15, PNC, 14; Shutterstock/Dmitry Kalinovsky, 1

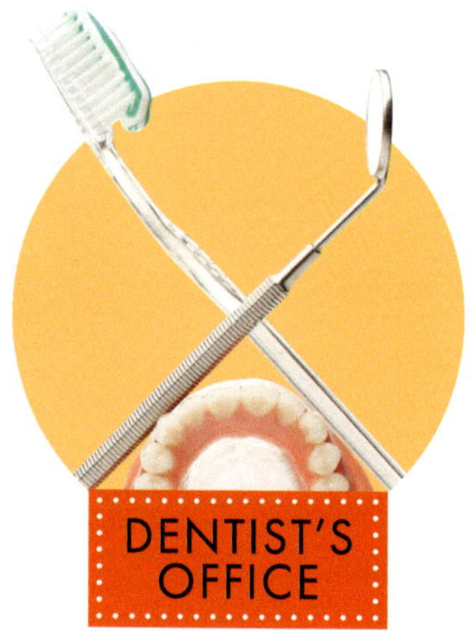